W9-BGZ-521

MANNERS
WITH FAMILY

JOSH PLATTNER

Consulting Editor, Diane Craig, M.A./Reading Specialist

Sandcastle

An Imprint of Abdo Publishing
abdopublishing.com

abdopublishing.com

Published by Abdo Publishing, a division of ABDO, PO Box 398166, Minneapolis, Minnesota 55439. Copyright © 2016 by Abdo Consulting Group, Inc. International copyrights reserved in all countries. No part of this book may be reproduced in any form without written permission from the publisher. SandCastle™ is a trademark and logo of Abdo Publishing.

Printed in the United States of America, North Mankato, Minnesota

062015
092015

THIS BOOK CONTAINS RECYCLED MATERIALS

Editor: Alex Kuskowski
Content Developer: Nancy Tuminelly
Cover and Interior Design and Production: Mighty Media, Inc.
Photo Credits: Shutterstock

Library of Congress Cataloging-in-Publication Data

Plattner, Josh, author.

Manners with family / Josh Plattner ; consulting editor, Diane Craig, M.A./Reading Specialist.

pages cm. -- (Manners)

Audience: PreK to grade 3.

ISBN 978-1-62403-718-4

1. Etiquette for children and teenagers--Juvenile literature. 2. Families--Juvenile literature. I. Title.

BJ1857.C5P535 2016

395.1'22--dc23

2014046375

SandCastle™ Level: Transitional

SandCastle™ books are created by a team of professional educators, reading specialists, and content developers around five essential components—phonemic awareness, phonics, vocabulary, text comprehension, and fluency—to assist young readers as they develop reading skills and strategies and increase their general knowledge. All books are written, reviewed, and leveled for guided reading, early reading intervention, and Accelerated Reader™ programs for use in shared, guided, and independent reading and writing activities to support a balanced approach to literacy instruction. The SandCastle™ series has four levels that correspond to early literacy development. The levels are provided to help teachers and parents select appropriate books for young readers.

EMERGING · BEGINNING · **TRANSITIONAL** · FLUENT

CONTENTS

MANNERS
WITH FAMILY

Manners are great! They help everyone get along. Use good manners with your family.

PRACTICE WITH PARENTS

Alex respects her parents.
She listens when they talk.
She says "I love you" too.

SUPER SIBLINGS

Eric hugs his brother.

They hang out together.

They listen to each other.

TAKING TURNS

Take turns with your **siblings**. Share things you both want to use. Be **polite** to each other.

GREAT GAMES

Playing games is fun.
Pick a game everyone in
the family likes to play.
Take turns choosing
the game.

NICE AND NEAT

David keeps his room neat. He makes his bed. He cleans up the house. He picks up every mess he makes.

TV TIME

Watch a show everyone likes. You can choose together. Try to keep quiet.

PLAY WITH ANIMALS

Be nice to your pets.

Treat them kindly.

Pet them gently.

CHORE CHAMPION!

Beth has **chores.** She does them to help out around the house. She doesn't **complain.**

KEEP IT UP!

Always practice good manners with
your family. Can you think of more?
What else could you do?

GLOSSARY

chore – a regular job or task, such as cleaning your room.

complain – to say you do not like something.

polite – having good manners or showing consideration for others.

sibling – a brother or sister.